FEATHERED FRIENDS

SPARROWS

Kim Thompson

NORWOOD HOUSE PRESS

Cataloging-in-Publication Data

Names: Thompson, Kim.
Title: Sparrows / Kim Thompson.
Description: Buffalo, NY : Norwood House Press, 2027. | Series: Feathered friends | Includes glossary and index.
Identifiers: ISBN 9781978580565 (pbk.) | ISBN 9781978580572 (library bound) | ISBN 9781978580589 (ebook)
Subjects: LCSH: Sparrows--Juvenile literature.
Classification: LCC QL696.T548 2027 | DDC 598.883--dc23

Published in 2027 by
Norwood House Press
2544 Clinton Street
Buffalo, NY 14224

Designer: Rhea Magaro
Editor: Tricia Hoffman

Photo credits: Cover, p.1 Wirestock Creators/Shutterstock.com; p.5 TAMER YILMAZ/Shutterstock.com; p.6 fluffandshutter/Shutterstock.com; p.7 Stephen A. Waycott/Shutterstock.com; p.8 Bachkova Natalia/Shutterstock.com; p.9 Robert Shupak/Shutterstock.com; p.10 Phillip van Zyl/Shutterstock.com; p.11 ISEN STOCKER/Shutterstock.com; p.13 alexkich/Shutterstock.com; p.14 Ramona Edwards/Shutterstock.com; p.15 Bob VonDrachek/Shutterstock.com; p.17 Fercast/Shutterstock.com; p.18 Gerardo Aguilar Anzures/Shutterstock.com; p.21 Kichigin/Shutterstock.com;

Printed in the United States of America

CPSIA compliance information: Batch #CSNHP27: For further information contact Norwood House Press at 1-800-237-9932.

TABLE OF CONTENTS

What Do Sparrows Look Like?

Sparrows are our feathered friends. There are many types of these small, grayish-brown songbirds. They are some of the most **common** birds in the world. All sparrows have cone-shaped **beaks** that are used to crush seeds.

The house sparrow is about as long as a dollar bill. It is brown on top with a gray belly.

Song sparrows can be slightly longer. They are reddish-brown. Their white bellies have dark streaks and spots.

Where Do Sparrows Live?

Sparrows live on every continent except Antarctica. About 40 sparrow **species** live in the United States.

Sparrows live all around. They are found in forests, grasslands, marshes, farms, and cities.

How Do Sparrows Grow Up?

Sparrows build nests from straw, twigs, feathers, and pieces of trash. Many nests are shaped like cups. Some have roofs.

House sparrows make nests under **eaves**, on street lights, and in birdhouses. They sometimes steal nesting sites from other birds.

Each summer, American tree sparrows lay a **clutch** of about five tiny eggs. It takes about 12 days for the eggs to **hatch**. For a few weeks, both parents feed the babies and keep them warm. Then, they are ready to fly away from the nest.

What Do Sparrows Eat?

Sparrows eat seeds and berries. They often visit bird feeders. Many sparrows also eat insects and spiders. In cities, sparrows eat crumbs on the sidewalk.

What Sounds Do Sparrows Make?

Sparrows make chirping sounds to give warnings and to protect their **territory**. Male sparrows sing to attract mates. Female song sparrows like males who have learned more complex songs.

Song sparrows living in different areas sing different songs. Their music has chirps, **trills**, and buzzes. They often perch on trees and wires as they sing.

What Funny Things Can Sparrows Do?

House sparrows take dust baths. They push their bellies into the dirt and toss dust over their backs. Then, they shake it off. This helps keep their feathers clean.

GLOSSARY

beaks (beeks): horny, pointed jaws on birds; bird bills

clutch (kluhch): all the eggs laid in a nest at the same time

common (KAH-muhn): found often and in large numbers; ordinary

eaves (eevz): the edges of a roof that hang over the sides of a building

hatch (hach): to break out of an egg to be born

species (SPEE-sheez): groups of living things that are alike and can reproduce together

territory (TER-i-tor-ee): an area that is defended by an animal and that often contains the animal's home

trills (trilz): times when a singer quickly goes back and forth between two different musical notes

THINKING QUESTIONS

1. What do all sparrows have in common?
2. Describe a house sparrow.
3. What do sparrows use to build nests?
4. What do sparrows eat?
5. Why do house sparrows take dust baths?

INDEX

ABOUT THE AUTHOR

Kim Thompson is a writer from Columbus, Ohio. She has written many books for kids. Lots of birds come to her backyard feeder. Her favorites are the showy red cardinals, tiny bright goldfinches, and waddling mallard ducks. Her two cats watch from the window.